ISBN: 9781593075552

黒鷺死体宅配便
the KUROSAGI corpse delivery service

1

story
EIJI OTSUKA

art
HOUSUI YAMAZAKI

original cover design
BUNPEI YORIFUJI

translation
TOSHIFUMI YOSHIDA

editor and english adaptation
CARL GUSTAV HORN

lettering and touch-up
IHL

contents

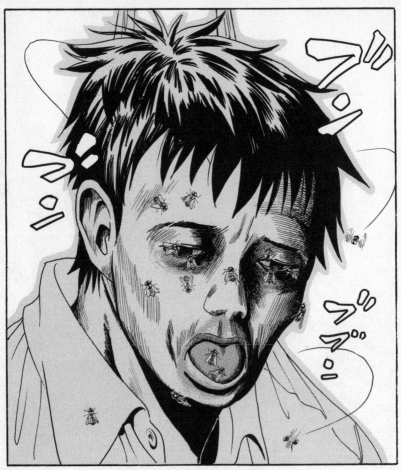

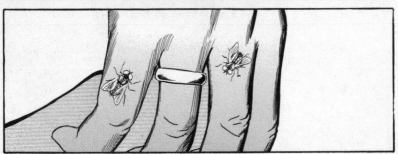

6

less than happy

1st delivery

しあわせ未満

Suicide Prevention
Message Box

Fuji Yoshida
Police Department
Suicide Prevention
Committee

WHY'D I EVEN BOTHER TO COME?

HEY!

OH MAN, I WISH I DIDN'T SEE THAT. HAIL AMIDA BUDDHA *NANMAIDA, NANMAIDA.*

REMEMBER...? WE'RE SUPPOSED TO BE GETTING OUR VOLUNTEER CREDITS SO WE CAN *GRADUATE*? HELP OUT THE POLICE, SAY A FEW PRAYERS FOR THE DEAD?

DON'T YOU THINK A BUDDHIST MAKING THE *SIGN OF THE CROSS* IS BAD FORM?

YEAH. WHY *DID* YOU COME OUT HERE?

HUH? OH... SEE, I DON'T REMEMBER THE *SUTRA* ALL THAT WELL, SO I THOUGHT I'D JUST THROW THAT IN.

OH...
YEAH.

MY NAME'S KURO KARATSU.

A FOURTH-YEAR STUDENT IN AN AVERAGE BUDDHIST UNIVERSITY.

AND THERE'S NOTHING SO COLD AS WINTER BREAK, YOUR SENIOR YEAR...

...WHEN YOU COUNT UP ALL YOUR AVERAGE GRADES, AND AVERAGE THEM OUT...TO AVERAGE.

AND YOU WONDER HOW YOU'RE GOING TO PAY FOR ALL YOUR WASTED TIME.

Contact (Kounozan Daiten-Ji)
☎ ▦▦ (▦▦▦) ▦▦▦ ▦ ▦▦

Wanted
-ka Shinri-kyo

Help Wanted

Shingen Sousou Main Temple

Monks in Training (▦▦▦▦▦▦▦▦)

Seeking In-House Monk!!
• Qualifications ▦▦▦▦ ▦▦ ▦▦ ▦▦▦▦▦
▦▦ ▦▦▦▦ ▦▦ ▦▦ ▦▦▦▦ ▦▦ ▦▦ ▦▦▦▦
• Salary ▦▦▦▦ ▦▦▦▦▦▦▦— ▦▦▦▦
• Location ▦▦ ▦▦▦▦▦▦▦ ▦▦▦▦▦▦▦
▦▦ ▦▦▦▦▦▦▦ ▦▦ ▦▦▦▦ ▦▦

CHANT SUTRAS IN AOKIGAHARA FOREST!

BE A VOLUNTEER!

HEH, EVEN THE VOLUNTEER JOBS ARE LIKE THIS.

DATE: 21ST DON'T FORGET YOUR BEADS!

NAMU!

let's go see some dead people!

DOESN'T ANYONE WANT, LIKE, AN OFFICE ASSISTANT? A FILE CLERK?

MAN, IT SUCKS BEING AN ENTRY-LEVEL BUDDHIST.

I could use some volunteer help...

YES, CAN YOU TELL? THEY'RE ALL MEMBERS OF MY GROUP.

LOOKS LIKE I'M NOT THE ONLY ONE YOU ROPED IN...

YEAH. MOST PEOPLE AT OUR SCHOOL, THEIR PARENTS RUN A TEMPLE OR SOMETHING...THEIR KIDS ARE GOING TO TAKE OVER SOMEDAY.

BUT ME AND MY FRIENDS, WE'RE LOOKING TO TAKE OUR EXPERIENCES HERE AT BUDDHIST COLLEGE, AND APPLY THEM TO THE REAL WORLD. WE'RE THINKING, THERE'S GOT TO BE OTHER WAYS TO MAKE MONEY OFF THIS.

SEE, WE'RE ALL A LITTLE DIFFERENT. WE DON'T COME FROM, UM, PRIESTLY FAMILIES...

OH... ME NEITHER.

OH, NUMATA? HE'S A DOWSER.

YOU KNOW, PEOPLE WHO USE A STICK OR A PENDULUM TO FIND WATER UNDERGROUND...?

FOR EXAMPLE, I TAKE PICTURES OF THE BODIES AND SELL THEM ON THE INTERNET.

JESUS!

Oops... sorry, I forgot.

UM... WHAT'S THAT TALL GUY DOING...?

COULDN'T HE JUST SMELL 'EM?

NUMATA USES HIS DOWSING TO FIND DEAD BODIES.

SHE DID THE STUDY ABROAD THING AND LEARNED EMBALMING. IT'S HARD TO FIND A SCHOOL THAT OFFERS IT HERE. THAT'S THE PROBLEM WITH JAPAN--IT'S ALWAYS CREMATION-- CRACKLE, CRACKLE, WOOSH, WOOSH.

AND THAT GIRL OVER THERE WORKING ON THE CORPSE IS LITTLE MAKINO.

16

HE SPEAKS TO THE ALIENS THROUGH HIS HAND PUPPET.

WHAT?

AND THE KID TALKING TO HIS HAND OVER THERE?

AH, THAT'S YATA. HE'S A CHANNELER.

THE ALIENS.

UH...WAIT A SEC--

I ALWAYS WONDERED WHERE THE "IN" CROWD HUNG.

WELL, THANKS FOR THE FIELD TRIP...

THAT'S RIGHT! I'M TALKIN' TO YOU, SKINHEAD! YOU DON'T BELIEVE I'M AN ALIEN, DO YOU?!

HEY YOU! BALDY!

WELL, I CALL BULLSHIT ON *THAT*, BUDDY! FOR *I* AM A SPACE ALIEN, AND MY *SPACE ALIEN SENSES* REVEAL *YOU* ARE DEFINITELY THE *WEIRDEST MOTHERFUCKER HERE!*

I KNOW WHAT *YOU'RE* THINKING! WOW, THESE GUYS ARE FREAKS, AND *I'M* SO NORMAL!

I-I'M SORRY...

...THAT WASN'T ME.

KARATSU...

HEY...WHAT DO YOU MEAN, ANYWAY? *HOW* AM I WEIRD?

BECAUSE WE'RE STANDING NEXT TO A *DEAD MAN!*

...BEHIND YOU...

YOU KNOW WHY FLIES KEEP TOUCHING US?

18

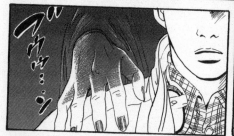

19

OKAY...

HA.

HOW LONG'S HE BEEN THERE?

...YOU CAUGHT ME.

WHAT WASN'T?

I MEAN, YEAH, I KNEW IT WASN'T NORMAL, BUT...

THAT I CAN HEAR THE VOICES OF THE DEAD.

WELL, KARATSU ... HE...

HEY! HEY, GUYS! DID YOU FIND ANOTHER ONE?

HE'S HAVING A CONVERSATION.

SO WHAT'S HE DOING?

AH. THAT'S HIM?

ピタ

IT'S NOT LIKE I WANT TO DO THIS...

SO THIS GUY KARATSU... HE'S AN *ITAKO*?

SO NOW WE GO LOOK FOR THE CORPSE'S GIRLFRIEND?

IT SOUNDED... INTERESTING.

THEN I GUESS WE HAVE TO FIND OUT WHO *HE* IS FIRST.

YOU DON'T KNOW?

WELL?

YEP.

HUH? IT WAS JUST A QUICK CHAT. YOU SERIOUS ABOUT THIS ...?

HE'S TRAPPED IN THAT BODY, ISN'T HE? HIS SOUL CAN'T MOVE ON WITHOUT HELP.

BUT YOU *ARE* HERE, AND I *BROUGHT* YOU HERE. AND NOW YOU'VE TOLD ALL OF US.

YOU DON'T HAVE TO. YOU WOULDN'T EVEN KNOW IF I WASN'T HERE.

...YES.

THEY TALK TO YOU BECAUSE YOU'RE THE KIND OF GUY WHO CAN'T SAY NO.

...

RIGHT. SO LET'S TAKE THIS HORRIBLE, STINKING, ROTTING THING BACK TO CAMPUS. QUICK, BEFORE THE COPS NOTICE.

BACK TO CAMPUS?!

KARATSU, THERE'S NOTHING IN THE HANDBOOK THAT SAYS STUDENTS CAN'T POSSESS CORPSES--OR, IN YOUR CASE, VICE-VERSA.

RESERVED FOR

山川家

WRITTEN ON BOARD: YAMAKAWA FAMILY

火葬棟
crematorium

IS THIS HOW IT IS, MR. YAMAKAWA?

...HOW WHAT IS?

26

YOU ONLY LOST A SINGER. YUKI IS MY OWN FLESH.

SHE'D ONLY HAD A RADIO SHOW LATELY...BUT WHAT ABOUT THE *REST* OF HER CAREER? YUKI WAS ON THE UPSWING, THAT'S THE WORST...SHE WAS GOING TO BE A BIG STAR, MR. YAMAKAWA... SHE...

HOW IT IS FOR *YUKI*...I-I MEAN...WHERE IS EVERYBODY...? JUST HER MANAGER AND HER DAD...? SHE DESERVED MORE THAN THIS, DAMNIT.

THAT BASTARD TOOK HER FROM ME.

...NEVER ENDED UP DEAD AND BURNED TO ASHES.

SHE SHOULD HAVE LISTENED TO ME AND NEVER COME TO THE CITY. NEVER MET THAT MAN...

I DON'T KNOW WHAT TO SAY...TO BE THAT LONELY...

YES.

I-I'M SORRY, MR. YAMAKAWA... I WAS LUCKY TO KNOW HER EVEN AS I DID...BUT YOUR FAMILY...I MEAN, IT WAS THE JUST THE TWO OF YOU, WASN'T IT?

WHAT DO YOU MEAN BY "STRANGE"?

1 0 3
KUROSAGI
VOLUNTEER SERVICE

THIS BODY ITSELF.

THERE'S EVIDENCE THAT THE BODY MOVED AFTER DEATH.

THE LIGATURE MARKS AND THE LIVIDITY OF THE ARMS AND LEGS SUGGESTS HE HUNG FOR AT LEAST TEN HOURS *POST MORTEM*.

NO--*IT* MOVED. WHEN WE FOUND THIS BODY, IT WAS LYING ON ITS STOMACH, A BROKEN ROPE AROUND THE NECK.

YOU MEAN *WAS* MOVED.

...AS IF HE DRAGGED HIMSELF ACROSS THE FOREST FLOOR.

SEE THE WAY THE BLOOD'S STILL POOLED IN HIS EXTREMITIES, NOT IN HIS BELLY. BUT THEN WE HAVE THESE SCRATCHES ON HIS HANDS, FULL OF DIRT AND MOSS...

HE WANTED TO MEET *YOU-U-U-U-U*, KARATSU...

OH! I KNOW!

COULD HIS SPIRIT HAVE DONE IT? TRYING TO MEET HIS LOVE?

30

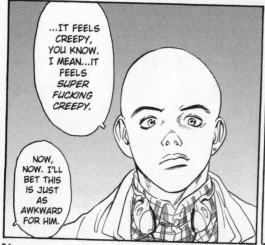

31

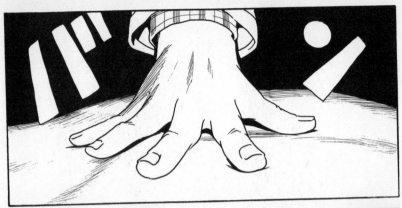

MY GIRL... FRIEND...IS YUKI... YAMA... KA...WA...

MY... NAMEIS... TOH...YA... FU...JISA... WA...

IT BROKE THE HEARTS OF ALL HER FANS...

SHE WAS A PERFORMER WHO CAME OUT OF THE TV DRAMAS. A PURE YOUNG IDOL, SHE EMBARKED UPON A MUSICAL CAREER...BUT TRAGICALLY, THE GROUP BROKE UP.

SO WHO WAS SHE...?

OH, YEAH... SHE WAS IN THAT GROUP, DOKKIKO.

TOUGH GUY LIKE YOU?

LOOK... LOOK INSIDE THE... THE... DID HE HAVE A *NOTEBOOK* ...?

NO...HE SAYS... THEY WERE... CHILDHOOD FRIENDS...

SO, THINK HE'S TELLING THE *TRUTH?* I MEAN, GUYS BOAST ALL THE TIME ABOUT CHICKS THEY NEVER HAD. THERE'S NO REASON TO THINK IT STOPS AT THE GRAVE.

OH, IT'S TRUE!

LET'S SEE.

WHY, YES HE DID.

...CLOSE ANY... MORE... COULDN'T BE...TO... GE...THER...

...SHE BE...CAME A STAR... WE COULD... N'T...BE...

HER FA... THER HATED... OUR LOVE E...VEN WORSE... WHEN...

34

WELL...THIS *IS* VOLUNTEER WORK...

...MAYBE GOOD DEEDS WILL BRING US LUCK.

HELLO...BOYS AND GHOULS OF...CORPSE CHAT. DO ANY OF YOU CREEPS KNOW...

KUROSAGI
Corpse Chat

Aosagi: Hello, boys and ghouls of Corpse Chat.
        Do any of you creeps know about Yuki|
Masaya: ru serious
Nono: The police and govt reccomend it lol
Yoshi: Yea I got a cpl volumes

Selly: so shes a dead
       idol???
Nono: Dokkiko yea
Selly: whose that
Aosagi: Anyone know?
>> Mr. Morgue has joined
/#CorpseChat

...ABOUT YUKI YAMAKAWA...AN IDOL SINGER FORMERLY OF THE GROUP DOKKIKO...SHE DIED RECENTLY...?

Mr. Morgue: Greetings, Aosagi, my fellow cadaveristic
            enthusiast! I indeed possess information on
            that decaying diva which may tickle your fancy!
Selly: i want to see dead idolz plz

UH-HUH ...

36

DID WE HAVE TO MEET UP AT THE STATION?

MAN, WHAT'S TAKING HER SO LONG?

WE CAN'T *AFFORD* ONE!

WELL, YOU KNOW, I RECOMMENDED WE RENT A CAR.

YEAH. WE DIDN'T BUY THE CORPSE A TICKET.

IS THERE A *LAW* AGAINST IT, YOU BALD-HEADED PRICK?

HEY... GUY-Y-Y-Y-YS... THAT OLD LADY OVER THERE KEEPS *LOOKING* AT US!

IS THAT SASAKI? IS SHE ON HER WAY?

THIS IS YATA. YEAH. YEAH. STILL DEAD. WHAT? YOU GOT HER HOME ADDRESS? GREAT!

...

SHE SAYS TO JUST GO ON WITHOUT HER...SHE'LL CATCH UP.

LOOK, ISN'T SHE BEING JUST A *LITTLE* BIT IRRESPONSIBLE? LEAVING IT ALL FOR US TO DEAL WITH?

OKAY... I'LL TRY.

YOU ACT LIKE DEATH IS HANGING OVER YOUR HEAD, KARATSU. TRY AND LOOK UP...AND THINK *POSITIVE!*

YEAH...LIKE, SHE'S PROBABLY FOLLOWING UP ON SOME SUPER-SECRET CLUES!

SHE'S ALWAYS BEEN THAT WAY. I WOULDN'T WORRY.

...BUT THIS ISN'T FROM HER BODY.

THE CREMATION RECEIPT SAYS YUKI YAMAKAWA...

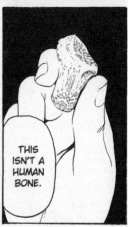

THIS ISN'T A HUMAN BONE.

SO HERE'S HER GRAVE...

WOW! THE FLOWERS ARE STILL FRESH.

YES. LET'S SET UP CAMP.

WELL, NOW WHAT? I DON'T THINK WE CAN RISK THIS IN BROAD DAYLIGHT...

WHAT? WE HAVE TO SLEEP OUT-DOORS? GROSS!

THIS WAY.

HEY! WE FOUND IT, YOU GUYS!

YOU SURE? THE LAST TWELVE FLIGHTS OF STAIRS WERE FALSE ALARMS!

YEAH... BE PREPARED, THAT'S WHAT WE ALWAYS USED TO SAY.

NUMACCHI, THAT'S SO COOL! YOU'RE LIKE A BOY SCOUT!

NO... IT'S NOT THAT...

WELL, WE *ARE* IN A GRAVEYARD. MAYBE EVERYONE'S JUST TALKING OVER HIM.

...YOU KNOW, I CAN'T *HEAR* HIM ANY LONGER. IT'S USUALLY LIKE...A KIND OF WHISPER YOU CAN'T QUITE MAKE OUT. BUT NOW I DON'T EVEN HEAR THAT.

GETTING ANY VIBES, KARATSU?

WE'RE ALL A LITTLE BEAT, KARATSU. WHY DON'T WE TAKE A NAP UNTIL MID-NIGHT? HE'S NOT GOING ANYWHERE.

43

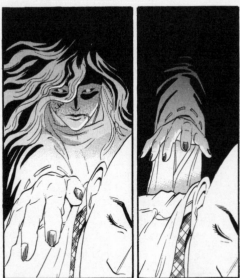

KURO...

WAKE UP, KURO ...

ガバ

EEEEEE!

...HEY! I WAS *TOTALLY* WRONG! WHERE'D HE GO?!

WHERE'D WHO GO? EWWW! I'VE GOT *BUG BITES!*

LOOK. I KNOW IT'S SPOOKY AROUND HERE. BUT...

THE GRAVE-YARD'S UP THE HILL...? THANK YOU.

SASAKI-SAN!?

UM...

HM? WHY AREN'T YOU WITH THE BODY?

WE WERE, BUT, IT, UH...GOT BORED, I GUESS.

WHAT DID YOU FIND OUT, SASAKI?

CHECK THIS OUT--THE PRIEST WHO DID THE SERVICES AT YUKI YAMAKAWA'S FUNERAL WAS FROM OUR SCHOOL.

NO...IT'S BECAUSE SHE WASN'T THERE...

SOMEONE SUBSTITUTED THE BODY OF A FAWN FOR YUKI YAMAKAWA'S.

HE TOOK ONE OF THE BONES HOME WITH HIM, AS A SORT OF, ER, SOUVENIR...

I TOOK A LOOK AT IT...IT WAS A DEER'S BONE.

...HER BODY IS SOMEWHERE NEARBY.

WELL, THAT MAKES OUR JOB A LITTLE SIMPLER. IF WE FIND HIM...

...WE'LL FIND HER AS WELL.

HE SAID *HE'D* LOVE YOU ALWAYS, DID HE?

DON'T YOU *KNOW* BOYS WILL TELL YOU THAT, YUKI? IT'S YOUR *DADDY* WHO LOVES YOU ALWAYS.

WHO'S THERE?!

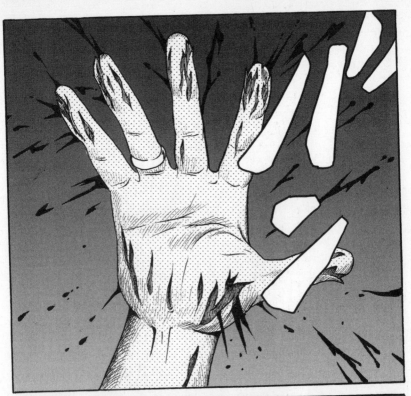

...GUN-SHOT?

THE BODY'S RIGHT THAT WAY. HMMM...MAYBE THE CORPSE WAS MISTAKEN FOR A BURGLAR.

TH-TH-THEN WHAT DOES IT MEAN?

I DON'T THINK SO. I MEAN, MOST PEOPLE WOULDN'T JUST SHOOT A BURGLAR, WOULD THEY?

...IT MEANS WE HAVE TO SEE FOR OURSELVES.

NO, LOOK. SOMEONE'S DEFINITELY BEEN HERE.

DOOR WAS OPEN... THE PLACE LOOKS ABANDONED.

WHO?

HELLO! IS ANYONE *HOME?*

TOHYA FUJISAWA. HMM. NORMALLY, THE DEAD BLEED VERY LITTLE...

KYAAA!

!!

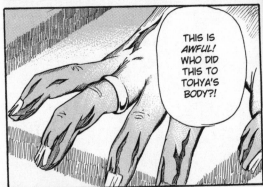

THIS IS *AWFUL!* WHO DID THIS TO TOHYA'S BODY?!

HE DID FIND HER.

choke

! ... YUKI YAMAKAWA.

WHAT THE HELL'S GOING ON HERE?

MAKINO ...?

... WHERE'D SHE GO ...?

THERE'S A *LIVING* MAN HERE WE NEED TO TALK TO.

DON'T
MOVE!

MAKINO
!

WE ASKED YOUR
DAUGHTER'S
BOYFRIEND, MR.
YAMAKAWA.

WHO THE
HELL ARE
YOU
KIDS?!

HOW DID
YOU KNOW
ABOUT...
US?

WELL... IT LOOKS LIKE YOU HAVE THE SAME PROBLEM, DON'T YOU...?

HE WON'T LEAVE HER ALONE!

BOYFRIEND? HE'S A MONSTER! HE CONVINCED MY YUKI TO KILL HERSELF! NOW LOOK AT HIM! LOOK AT HIM!

IT WAS JUST THE TWO OF US IN THIS HOUSE, YEAR AFTER YEAR...NIGHT AFTER NIGHT.

PROBLEM? SHE NEVER HAD A PROBLEM WITH IT, I ASSURE YOU.

I MADE HER HAPPY!

YOU DON'T UNDER-STAND!

SHUT UP!

WORLD'S GREATEST DAD.

ADMIT IT, MR. YAMAKAWA. YOU LIKE HER BETTER THIS WAY. NOW SHE'S EVEN LESS OF A PERSON TO YOU.

KARATSU?

BUT IT'S REALLY SAD THAT ONCE YUKI GOT AWAY FROM YOU, SHE COULDN'T WAIT TO COMMIT SUICIDE, ISN'T IT?

NO... NOT ME...

YOU'RE DEAD!

WH-WHAT THE HELL ARE YOU BABBLING ABOUT...?

STOP HURTING THE DEAD. I CAN HEAR THEIR VOICES.

YOU
AGAIN
...

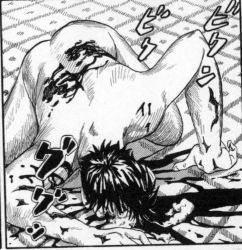

STAY DEAD!

M-
MONSTER...
MONSTER...

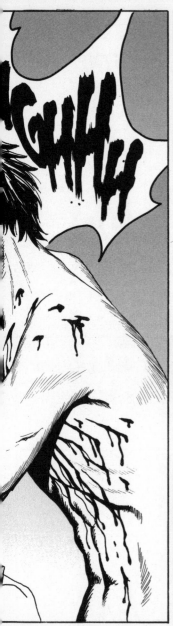

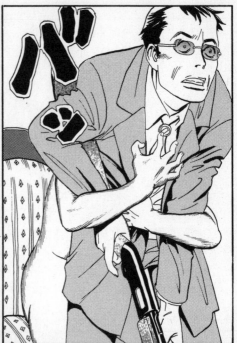

...Yuki?

...WOULD SOMEONE TELL ME WHAT JUST HAPPENED...?

SO YOU DON'T REMEMBER A THING AFTER HE TOOK MAKINO HOSTAGE...?

I WONDER IF IT WAS THEIR RESTLESS SPIRITS THAT MADE THOSE CORPSES MOVE...OR IF IT WAS KARATSU HERE.

AH... NOPE.

NOPE.

SO, ANY NEWS?

NEVER MIND.

EXCUSE ME?

WHAT THE--?!

WHAT THE WHAT?

YOU CAN GO TELL THE COPS ABOUT TONIGHT'S FESTIVAL OF FUCKED-UP SHIT IF YOU WANT, BUT I'M STAYING RIGHT HERE ON YATA'S ARM...WHERE IT'S SAFE!

HOW WOULD THERE BE *NEWS*? WE BURIED THEM TOGETHER IN THE FOREST.

THREE MILLION YEN.

THE LOTTERY TICKET...IT'S A WINNING NUMBER...

I'LL TAKE THAT.

HEY...NOT *BAD!* SPLIT FIVE WAYS, THAT'S 600 THOUSAND YEN APIECE!

LET ME SEE!

WHAT? REALLY?!

WE CAN'T GO AROUND EXPLAINING TO PEOPLE WHAT WE CAN DO...LET ALONE GET PAID FOR DOING IT.

NOT TO *LIVING* PEOPLE, THAT IS. BUT A *DEAD* MAN NOT ONLY CONFIDED IN US, HE ARRANGED A KARMIC PAYOFF.

HUNDREDS OF PEOPLE DIE IN THIS COUNTRY EVERY DAY. HOW MANY DIE THE WAY THEY WANTED TO...WITH ALL THEIR WISHES FULFILLED?

I SAY WE USE THIS MONEY AS START-UP CAPITAL...AND FIND THE OTHERS ALL AROUND US WHO NEED A LAST SERVICE FOR THEIR BODIES...

...THE KUROSAGI CORPSE DELIVERY SERVICE.

OH, YEAH... RIGHT.

BECAUSE WE'RE ALL COMPLETELY UNEMPLOY- ABLE?

TELL ME AGAIN...WHY'D WE AGREE TO HER IDEA...?

In days of old, it was said that when the elderly reached the age of sixty, they would be left in a place called Dendera Field to die.

The original Dendera Field was located in Aozasa Village. But every town would set aside their own plot for the purpose...

—from *Tales of Tono* by Kunio Yanagita

AND THIS IS DENDERA FIELD...

HUH. I ALWAYS HEARD THEY DROPPED THEM ON A MOUNTAIN TO DIE.

IT'S SORT OF A HILL THINGIE.

I DUNNO. PEOPLE WERE A LOT SHORTER BACK THEN. MAYBE THIS QUALIFIED.

ANYWAY, I GUESS WE CAN LEAVE THAT HERE, RIGHT?

OH YEAH. RIGHT...

...HEY, ISN'T THIS LIKE, A HISTORIC SITE OR SOMETHING? WHAT IF WE RUN INTO SOME TOURISTS?

MY NAME IS KURO KARATSU. WHEN I TOUCH THEM, THE DEAD SPEAK TO ME.

WELL, THE CUSTOMER IS ALWAYS RIGHT.

I GUESS.

SHOULD WE SAY A PRAYER?

THAT'S WHAT BRINGS US TO DENDERA FIELD.

DENDERA FIELD

THIS ONE IS INSIDE THAT ALTAR.

WE CALL OURSELVES THE KUROSAGI CORPSE DELIVERY SERVICE, AND OUR CLIENTS ARE TO BE FOUND EVERYWHERE.

BINGO!

ｸﾝ
ｸﾝ
ｸﾝ

IT ALL STARTED WHEN NUMATA FOUND THE BODY. YOU KNOW THOSE PLACES THAT HAVE A SIGN, "NO TRASH DUMPING"?

CORPSE AHOY!

...HUH? WHAT'S THE MATTER?

THAT'S WHERE SHE WAS... DOWN IN THERE.

MAYBE THE RAT CAME LOOKING FOR THE FOOD OFFERING AND GOT STUCK INSIDE?

WHY ARE WE EVEN *HERE*? IF IT'S, LIKE, A DEAD RAT OR SOMETHING, I'M GOING TO BE REALLY MAD.

I HOPE THAT'S JUST THE TRASH...

LOOK, MY PENDULUM SWINGS A WHOLE DIFFERENT WAY FOR DEAD RATS. I'M TELLING YOU, THERE'S A *BODY* INSIDE.

WHY WOULD SOMEONE STICK A CORPSE INSIDE A FAMILY ALTAR?

DON'T FORCE IT! DEAD RATS WILL FLY ALL OVER!

WOULDN'T YOU KNOW, IT'S LOCKED.

What the hell is a "rat-man"?

Maybe it's some kind of rat-man.

C'MON, LET'S NOT FIGHT. WE'LL JUST TAKE A LOOK INSIDE AND SETTLE THIS.

I'M TELLING YOU, IT'S NOT A--

NOW...

...AREN'T YOU SORRY YOU EVER DOUBTED ...?

YOU WANT ME TO...ASK HER? WELL...

THEY PROBABLY DIDN'T KNOW WHAT DAY TO PUT IT OUT.

AN ILLEGALLY DUMPED MUMMY.

WELL, I'VE DONE MY PART. TIME FOR YOU TO DO YOUR THING, SHAMAN KING.

SHUT UP, MAN.

YEAH-- BETTER SUCK THAT FINGER *BEFORE*, NOT AFTER.

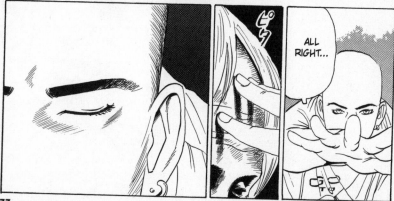

ALL RIGHT...

HUH? THAT'S IT?

T... AKEM... ETO... DEN... DERA...

"TAKE ME TO DENDERA." WHERE'S THAT?

WHAT'D SHE SAY...?

SOUNDS LIKE A TEMPLE.

OLD PEOPLE MUMBLE SOMETIMES.

DENDERA... DENDERA...CAN'T FIND ANYTHING BY THAT NAME. DO YOU THINK WE HEARD IT RIGHT?

LISTEN, MR. MY-KARMA-IS-OH-SO-SPOTLESS, WE'RE RUNNING A *BUSINESS* HERE, NOT A CHARITY. DID YOU CHECK THE CORPSE'S CREDIT?

LOOK, IT COULDN'T BE HELPED. I COULD ONLY GET FOUR WORDS OUT OF HER.

HEY...I *TOLD* YOU HOW WE WERE GOING TO DO THIS, KARATSU. YOU DON'T BRING ANY BODIES HERE BEFORE YOU DISCUSS HOW THEY'RE GOING TO PAY!

WELL, I SUPPOSE SO YOU CAN CARRY IT. FORTUNATELY SHE'S ALL DRIED OUT.

HEY, YOU LOOK COOL WITH THAT, NUMATA. JUST LIKE A WANDERING MONK.

AND WHY...DOES THAT ALTAR HAVE CARRYING STRAPS ON IT...?

R-REALLY...?

WELL, I SUPPOSE IT'S TO AID IN TOTING THE CORPSE. YES, SHE'S LIGHT, BUT KIND OF BENT INTO THAT AWKWARD SHAPE.

YEAH. SHE'S GOT YOU THERE.

AND WHY...WOULD YOU EVEN NEED TO?

LIKE IN THE OLD DAYS...TO UBA SUTE YAMA...

RIGHT, RIGHT, THE MOUNTAIN WHERE YOU THROW AWAY OLD PEOPLE.

WHAT...YOU THINK SOMEONE HAULED HER OFF TO DIE?

IT'S IN TONO...IN IWATE PREFECTURE! WE HAVEN'T EVEN GOTTEN *TRAIN FARE* YET OUT OF THIS PRUNE!

HOW FAR IS THAT, EXACTLY? I MEAN, I'M OKAY WITH IT FOR THE MOMENT, BUT IT'S STARTING TO CHAFE A LITTLE.

NOT DENDERA TEMPLE! *DENDERA FIELD!* THAT WAS ANOTHER NAME FOR THE MOUNTAIN!

I read it in *Tono Monogatari* by Kunio Yanagita!

WAIT A SECOND...

THE ALTAR'S MADE OF EBONY WITHOUT THE USE OF GOLD LEAF. BUT IT'S WELL CONSTRUCTED, AND UTILIZES THE NATURAL LUSTER OF THE WOOD. VERY GOOD WORKMANSHIP, OVERALL.

Whoa! It's like Antiques Roadshow!

HEY. CAN WE KEEP THE BOX SHE CAME IN?

WELL, *ALL RIGHT!* LET'S *GO*, GANG!

REALLY ?!

YOU KNOW, IF WE AIR IT OUT A LITTLE AND SELL IT ON THE INTERNET, I'LL BET WE COULD GET 500,000 YEN.

RIGHT, SO HERE WE ARE. NOW ALL WE'VE GOT TO DO IS TAKE HER OUT OF THE ALTAR, AND WE CAN GO HOME.

IT'S WHAT SHE WANTS ANYWAY, NUMATA. NO REASON TO BE UPSET ABOUT IT.

B-BUT...

HM? WHAT'S THE MATTER, NUMATA...?

....

WE'RE NOT *REALLY* GOING TO LEAVE HER HERE, ARE WE?! POOR GRANDMA!

HEY! REMEMBER YOUR BUDDHIST PRINCIPLES OF *NON-ATTACHMENT*! LET'S DUMP HER AND GET BACK TO CAMPUS!

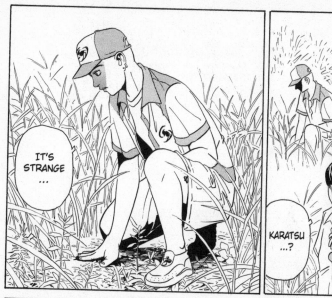

IT'S STRANGE ...

WHAT SHOULD WE DO, KARATSU ...?

KARATSU ...?

MAYBE IT WAS JUST A LEGEND.

THERE'S SOME RESIDUAL PRESENCE FROM SPIRITS...BUT I'M NOT SENSING ANY THOUGHTS FROM THE DEAD HERE.

WHAT IS?

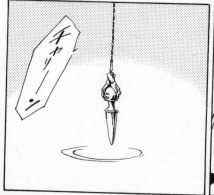

BUT...THIS *IS* THE PLACE IN THE BOOK, RIGHT?

WAIT A SEC...MAYBE I GOT IT WRONG...

HUH?

HE'S RIGHT...I'M NOT GETTING ANYTHING EITHER.

BUT THEN HE SAYS HERE IN CHAPTER 268, *"THERE IS ALSO A DENDERA FIELD IN TSUCHIBUCHI VILLAGE'S AZATAKAMURO...EACH VILLAGE HAD ITS OWN DENDERA FIELD SPECIFIED FOR THAT PURPOSE..."*

KUNIO YANAGITA WROTE ABOUT THIS PLACE HERE...AOZASA VILLAGE IN TONO. THAT'S WHY THE TOURISTS COME TO VISIT, BECAUSE *TONO MONOGATARI* MADE IT FAMOUS.

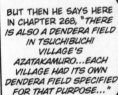

...IF I READ THIS RIGHT, MAYBE ALL OVER NORTH-EASTERN JAPAN.

THERE COULD BE "DENDERA FIELDS" ALL OVER THIS AREA...

YOU SEE WHAT I MEAN...? IT'S LIKE IT'S A GENERIC NAME.

YOU WEREN'T?

OH, NO, MISTER... WE WEREN'T GOING TO THROW THIS AWAY!

D-D-DUMPING?

UM...YEAH... RIGHT...

right?

NO! ACTUALLY, IT'S THE OTHER WAY ROUND. YOU SEE, WE'RE *STUDENT VOLUNTEERS,* COME HERE TO *PICK UP TRASH* AND *KEEP TONO BEAUTIFUL!*

YOU MISSED SOME.

OH! REALLY? WOW! HOW'D WE MISS ALL *THAT?*

OKAY, GANG-- LET'S GO DISPOSE OF THIS ALTAR SOMEONE THOUGHTLESSLY ABANDONED!

I'M IMPRESSED.

WAIT!

ARE YOU THE SAME GIRL WHO CHEERILY EMBALMS TWO-WEEK-OLD CORPSES?

...OH. *HERE.*

SO FAR, NONE OF THIS TRASH SEEMS TO BE LINKED TO THE OLD WOMAN.

I THINK HE'S TAKING THIS FAR TOO PER-SONALLY.

YEAH! GRANDMA'S BOY!

DON'T YOU GUYS FEEL SORRY FOR HER?

WELL, KEEP LOOK-ING!

88

UM, SORRY... THAT WASN'T ME.

WHAT PEOPLE?

HEY! *RETARDS!* TRASH DON'T TALK! MAYBE IT *BUZZES* SOMETIMES, BUT IT DON'T TALK! YOU GOTTA ASK THE PEOPLE WHO *DUMPED* THIS SHIT!

THOSE PEOPLE!

Oh, shit.

Hey, look!

UH-OH. THEY SEEM TO HAVE NOTICED US.

IF THEY ARE, THEN THEY'D KNOW WHERE GRANDMA CAME FROM!

THEY THE ONES WHO'VE BEEN TOSSING ALL THIS?

SOME FREAK'S RUNNING UP THE HILL! START THE TRUCK!

O-OKAY!

WAIT! I GOT A QUESTION!

HE'S COMING STRAIGHT FOR US!

WAIT! WAIT!

--WAIT!

I SAID--

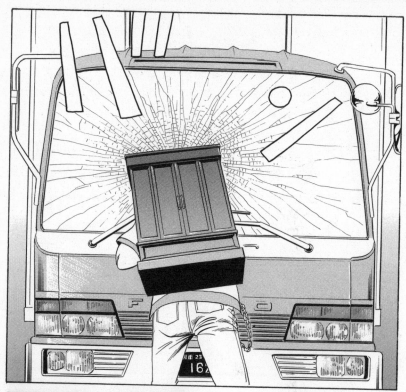

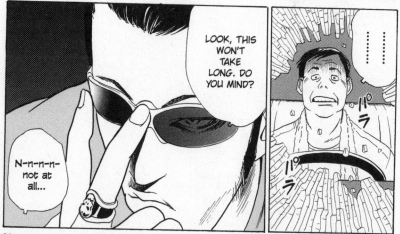

R-RIGHT...

WELL, THEY WERE NICE AND FORTHCOMING, WEREN'T THEY?

ゴ

YOU KNOW, NUMATA, YOU HAVE A WAY ABOUT YOU.

YEAH, KARATSU... WOULDN'T YOU RATHER POKE AROUND INSIDE A RICKETY OLD BUILDING THAN A SMELLY GARBAGE DUMP?

DO WE GO THERE? HOW ARE WE SUPPOSED TO FIND OUT ANYTHING IF WE DON'T GO THERE?

WELL, TO BE HONEST...

ANYWAY, NOW WE KNOW THE TRASH CAME FROM AN APARTMENT THAT'S BEEN CONDEMNED... SO, DO WE GO THERE?

SO, THIS IS THE ROOM SHE LIVED IN...

YEAH, SHE HAD A SON AND TWO GRANDSONS ABOUT ELEMENTARY SCHOOL AGE...

DID YOU SAY "FAMILY"?

I FIGURED IT'D BE OLD, BUT THIS PLACE IS ANCIENT...

I TALKED TO THE LANDLORD AND ACCORDING TO HIM, THE PLACE IS ALMOST SIXTY YEARS OLD. ONE ROOM WITH A SHARED BATH WAS ONLY 8000 YEN A MONTH...BUT THE OLD LADY'S FAMILY COULD BARELY EVEN AFFORD THAT.

AND THE LANDLORD SAID HE HADN'T SEEN THE GRANDMA FOR AT LEAST A YEAR BEFORE THAT...

WE DON'T KNOW. THE REST OF THE FAMILY DISAPPEARED TWO MONTHS AGO. NO FORWARDING ADDRESS.

SO HER SON LOCKED HER INSIDE THE ALTAR.

IN ANY EVENT, BY THE TIME THE LANDLORD CAME TO CHECK, THEY WERE LONG GONE...

HUH?

NUMATA... PUT THE GRANDMA DOWN. I WANT TO TRY AGAIN.

· · · · ·

THEN I GUESS THAT MEANS WE'RE AT ANOTHER DEAD END.

YOU KNOW...DO MY *THING*.

I...I DON'T CARE! I'LL CARRY GRANDMA NO MATTER HOW LONG IT TAKES!

OKAY...

THIS IS DIFFERENT FROM BEFORE ...

!

ピクッ

YES.

SHE MUST HAVE SEEN SOMEONE ELSE DO THIS LONG AGO...WHEN SHE WAS A CHILD.

IS THIS A VISION OF HERS... OF THE CORPSE ...?

AND SO...

YEARS LATER.

SHE'S OLD NOW. THIS IS HER CHILD.

98

KARATSU!
KARATSU!

...KARATSU?

...I'VE NEVER SEEN THEIR *MEMORIES* BEFORE...IT'S STRANGE...

I SAW THE VILLAGE WHERE SHE GREW UP. THEY MUST HAVE HAD THE SAME CUSTOM THERE, THEIR OWN DENDERA FIELD...SHE STILL REMEMBERED. SO SHE WANTED TO BE TAKEN THERE.

"IN THE OLD WAY"?

SHE WASN'T MURDERED. SHE PUT *HERSELF* IN THE ALTAR SO THAT THERE WOULD BE ONE LESS MOUTH TO FEED. AND SHE ASKED TO BE CAST OFF...IN THE OLD WAY.

THAT PLACE UP IN TONO...I DIDN'T SENSE THE DEAD THERE. AND NEITHER DID YOU.

WELL, THEN THAT'S WHAT SHE WANTS! LET'S DO IT, THEN!

WE CAN'T!

BUT...

WE CAN'T.

IT'S JUST A STORY IN THE OLD BOOKS NOW. PEOPLE DON'T ABANDON THEIR PARENTS AND GRANDPARENTS IN *FIELDS* ANYMORE! SHE WANTS THAT MEMORY BECAUSE SHE THOUGHT IT WAS...IT WAS A PROPER ENDING. THAT'S WHAT SHE WANTS.

EVEN IF WE COULD FIGURE OUT EXACTLY WHICH VILLAGE SHE CAME FROM...IT WOULDN'T REALLY BE THE PLACE SHE WANTS TO GO.

......

BUT...WHAT DO WE DO WITH HER NOW...?

SOMEWHERE THAT PEOPLE CAST THINGS OFF IS ABOUT AS CLOSE AS WE CAN COME.

WHAT ELSE CAN WE DO? THE PLACE WHERE SHE WANTS TO GO IS THE DENDERA FIELD OF HER MEMORIES. BUT THERE'S NO SUCH PLACE TODAY.

WHY HERE, KARATSU?

......

I JUST FEEL THIS PLACE IS RIGHT...

HEY...TAKE A LOOK AT THAT!

HUH? IS THAT A *HOUSE*? NO...

!!

DEN TERA... "DEN TEMPLE."

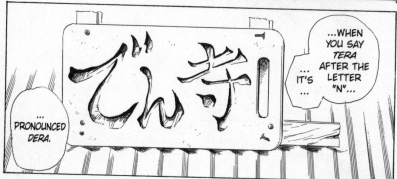

...WHEN YOU SAY *TERA* AFTER THE LETTER "N"...

IT'S...

...PRONOUNCED DERA.

WHAT ARE *YOU* DOING HERE?

HUH ?!

WHAT'S ALL THIS NOISE SO EARLY IN THE MORNING?

WELL, UM, ER...

アワフワ

THIS IS MY TEMPLE.

I LIVE HERE. WHAT ARE *YOU* DOING HERE?

Whatever happened to keeping Tono beautiful?

SO--LOOKING FOR A PLACE TO LEAVE THE ELDERLY, HUH?

heh--heh--heh--heh...

WOW! HOW COULD YOU TELL?

NUMATA! YOU'RE SUPPOSED TO DENY EVERYTHING!

HEY, BIG GUY. YOU'RE NOT CARRYING A *CORPSE* AROUND IN THAT ALTAR, ARE YOU?

104

TONO IS MY HOME TOWN. I GO BACK THERE TO SEE DENDERA SOMETIMES.

BUT THAT PLACE IS ONLY A SIGN IN A FIELD NOW. THE REAL *UBA SUTE YAMA* IS...

WELL. COME ON.

HUH? HEY...

I DON'T KNOW...AND IS THAT GUY *REALLY* A MONK?

WHAT'S GOING ON?

LOTS OF THEM?

BUT I'M GETTING A READING... THERE'S BODIES HERE.

LOTS OF THEM.

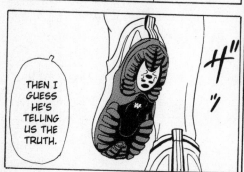

THEN I GUESS HE'S TELLING US THE TRUTH.

YOU FOUND IT AT LAST.

...WHY IS IT IN THE MIDDLE OF TOKYO...?

DENDERA FIELD.

TONO IS A TOURIST SPOT.

WHERE DO PEOPLE LIVE AND DIE THESE DAYS? IN THE CITIES. AND SO THE STORY OF DENDERA FIELD CONTINUES HERE.

SO YOU CREATED A DENDERA FIELD... HERE...?

PEOPLE THINK IT'S JUST A STORY IN THE OLD BOOKS. BUT IT'S SOMETHING PEOPLE DO EVERY DAY. I FOUND ALL THESE DEAD DUMPED IN TRASH AND LANDFILLS...JUST LIKE YOU DID.

IT WAS ALREADY HERE. SIX HUNDRED AND THIRTY THOUSAND ELDERLY PEOPLE LIVE ON THEIR OWN IN TOKYO ALONE.

• • • • • • •

I JUST TRY TO BRING A LITTLE DIGNITY TO IT. LEAVE HER WITH ME. I'LL PRAY FOR HER.

2nd delivery: lonely people —— the end

HEY, HAVE YOU HEARD THIS RUMOR?

HE PICKS UP THIS GIRL BY ASKING, "MISS, WOULD YOU LIKE A FREE CUT?"

WELL, THIS REAL GOOD-LOOKING GUY, HE SAYS HE RUNS A BEAUTY SALON...

WHAT... ANOTHER SCARY STORY?

SHE STARTS TO THINK SOMETHING IS STRANGE... BUT SITS DOWN... AND GETS DROWSY...

SHE FALLS ASLEEP. AND THEN A FEW HOURS LATER--

SO, SHE GOES ALONG WITH HIM, AND FINDS HERSELF IN AN EMPTY ROOM WITH A SINGLE CHAIR.

GHHHHH

MMMH

MMH

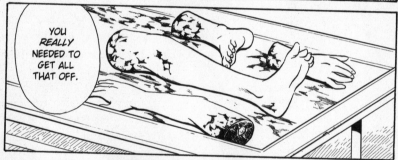

YOU *REALLY* NEEDED TO GET ALL THAT OFF.

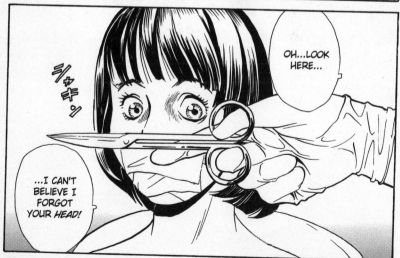

OH...LOOK HERE...

...I CAN'T BELIEVE I FORGOT YOUR *HEAD!*

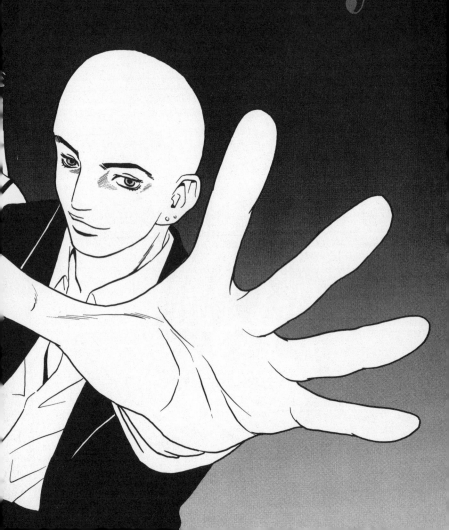

magician of lost love

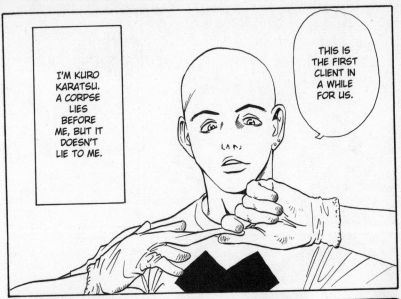

THIS IS THE FIRST CLIENT IN A WHILE FOR US.

I'M KURO KARATSU. A CORPSE LIES BEFORE ME, BUT IT DOESN'T LIE TO ME.

IT TELLS ME ITS TROUBLES AND ITS CARES.

WE MAKE A LIVING OFF THESE DEAD, MY FRIENDS AND I.

...KEEPS ITS SOUL BOUND TO THIS FLESH.

ALL THE THINGS THAT MAKE IT REST UNEASY...

KEIKO MAKINO, A LITTLE WEIRDO WHO'S STUDIED MORTUARY SCIENCE IN AMERICA.

YUJI YATA, WHO RECEIVES STRANGE FOUL-MOUTHED INTELLIGENCES FROM AN ALIEN THROUGH HIS HAND PUPPET.

MAKOTO NUMATA, A DOWSER WHO CAN'T FIND A DROP OF WATER BUT WHOSE PENDULUM SEEKS OUT CORPSES LIKE A BLOWFLY.

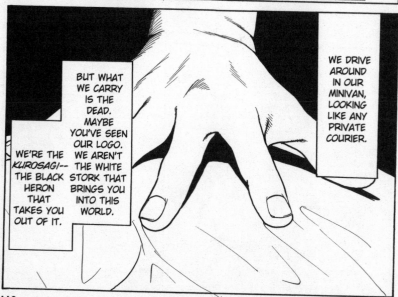

WE'RE THE *KUROSAGI*-- THE BLACK HERON THAT TAKES YOU OUT OF IT.

BUT WHAT WE CARRY IS THE DEAD. MAYBE YOU'VE SEEN OUR LOGO. WE AREN'T THE WHITE STORK THAT BRINGS YOU INTO THIS WORLD.

WE DRIVE AROUND IN OUR MINIVAN, LOOKING LIKE ANY PRIVATE COURIER.

HMM?

AND THE KEY TO OUR OPERATION IS MY ABILITY. WITHOUT IT, NONE OF THIS WOULD BE POSSIBLE...

OR SO I THOUGHT...

AND WHAT'S SHE GOT? HOW MUCH DOES SHE HAVE?

SO WHAT'S SHE WANT? WHAT DOES SHE NEED?

WHO?

IT'S FROM AN OLD MANGA.

TAKE DOWN THEIR ORDERS? WHO DO YOU THINK I AM? SABURO?

HEY, WHAT GOOD ARE YOU IF YOU CAN'T EVEN TAKE DOWN THEIR ORDERS PROPERLY?!

LOOK, DO YOU WANT ME TO HEAR YOU, OR *HER*?

DON'T BE SILLY!

HEY! YOU KIDS! WHAT'S ALL THE NOISE? FIND A DEAD BODY OR SOMETHING?

バタン

ギックゥ

BROUGHT ANOTHER UNIDENTIFIED BODY BACK TO SCHOOL?

103
KUROSAGI
VOLUNTEER SERVICE

SHE'S THE CHAIR OF OUR CAMPUS VOLUNTEER GROUP--WHICH SHE QUICKLY TURNED INTO A MONEYMAKING OPERATION. SHE CAME UP WITH THE NAME OF OUR COMPANY...AND LIKES TO GIVE IT ORDERS.

MAKINO SAID SHE HAD SOME FRESHENING UP TO DO.

FRESHENING UP?

...SO WHAT ARE YOU ALL DOING OUT HERE?

OH YEAH, I FORGOT. THIS IS AO SASAKI.

LISTEN HERE. IT DOESN'T JUST PROTECT THE CORPSE, IT PROTECTS YOU.

IT'S SPECIAL, ALL RIGHT.

YOU MEAN EMBALMING. YOU SHOULD RESPECT HER SPECIALTY.

122

IT STOPS BACTERIA FROM USING THE CORPSE AS FOOD. THAT'S WHAT PUTREFACTION *IS*, YOU KNOW...

IN OTHER COUNTRIES, WHEN THEY NEED TO MOVE A BODY, OR WANT IT TO BE VIEWED BEFORE A BURIAL, THEY USE EMBALMING TO PRESERVE THE CORPSE'S APPEARANCE. BUT IT HAS A PUBLIC HEALTH ROLE, TOO.

BUT IF IT'S SO DANGEROUS, IS IT SAFE TO LET MAKINO HANDLE IT ON HER OWN?

A SMALL AMOUNT OF CONTACT IS FINE.

I'VE GOT TO *TOUCH* THEM...

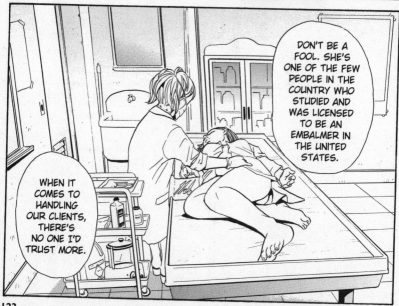

DON'T BE A FOOL. SHE'S ONE OF THE FEW PEOPLE IN THE COUNTRY WHO STUDIED AND WAS LICENSED TO BE AN EMBALMER IN THE UNITED STATES.

WHEN IT COMES TO HANDLING OUR CLIENTS, THERE'S NO ONE I'D TRUST MORE.

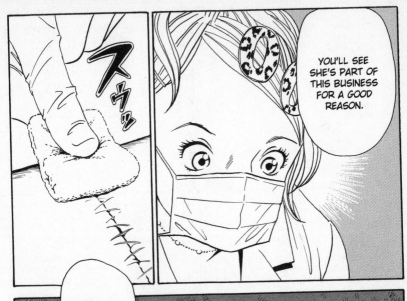

YOU'LL SEE SHE'S PART OF THIS BUSINESS FOR A GOOD REASON.

SOUNDS LIKE MAKINO'S FINISHING UP IN THERE.

MORGUE

HERE... TAKE A LOOK.

IT'S NOT REALLY A BODY...

MORGUE

UH... WELL... HOW DID IT GO...?

DID YOU TAKE CARE OF THE BODY?

124

THOSE SCARS... WHAT HAPPENED TO HER?

SHE'S NOT A DEAD PERSON.

...THEY'RE SEWINGS.

THEY'RE NOT SCARS...

LOOK CARE-FULLY.

THE SKIN ON EACH SIDE OF THE JOIN...

HA.

IT WASN'T ALL YOUR DIFFERENT VOICES I WAS HEARING. THEY WERE ALL COMING FROM *HER*.

コキッ

IT WAS A PROFESSIONAL JOB. GLUTARALDEHYDE AND ALKYLATING AGENTS IN THE ARTERIES...THE LIMBS WERE MASSAGED TO REMOVE RIGOR...

SOMEONE *ALREADY* EMBALMED HER.

THAT'S NOT ALL...SHE WAS WELL PRESERVED WHEN WE FOUND HER.

I THINK WHOEVER EMBALMED HER STITCHED THEM UP...AND WHOEVER EMBALMED HER, KILLED THEM ALL.

NOT A LOT OF GUYS KNOW HOW TO DO THIS IN JAPAN.

127

BUT OUR JOB IS TO DELIVER CORPSES... NOT TO PLAY DETECTIVE.

CAN WE DELIVER IT, THOUGH? I MEAN, WHICH ONE?

WHY DON'T WE TAKE OUT THE STITCHES AND DELIVER THEM SEPARATELY?

ALL RIGHT, WE'LL PRETEND WE NEVER FOUND HER. I MEAN, THEM.

WHAT DO YOU THINK SHE IS, A MODEL KIT?

sigh

WHAT IF WE JUST DELIVER ONE, BUT ASK A BONUS FOR EXTRA PARTS RECEIVED?

WE'D GET ARRESTED...

WHAT? KNOCK, KNOCK, HELLO...WE BROUGHT YOUR DAUGHTER'S ARM?

Y-YEAH.

YOU'LL HELP ME WITH THAT... RIGHT, MAKINO-CHAN?

MAKINO AND I WILL FIND OUT WHO PUT THEM TOGETHER.

THIS IS WHAT WE'LL DO. YATA, NUMATA, YOU SHUT UP. KARATSU, TRY TO GET A VOICE FROM EACH OF THEM.

128

HANDSOME, EH? AND WHAT WAS YOUR RELATIONSHIP...?

R-R-RELATIONSHIP...?

OH, SO YOU DIDN'T DO HIM?

MORE LIKE A BIG BROTHER.

HE WAS THE ONLY OTHER JAPANESE THERE THAT YEAR...SO NATURALLY, WE TALKED A LOT. HE WAS A TOP STUDENT...I KIND OF LOOKED UP TO HIM.

SORRY TO KEEP YOU WAITING.

NO, I DIDN'T DO HIM--

AND YOU SEEM AS ENERGETIC AS EVER, MAKINO-KUN. HOW LONG HAS IT BEEN...?

...NICE TO MEET YOU.

MY NAME IS SASAKI...I'M AN UPPER-CLASSMAN OF HERS AT THE UNIVERSITY...

AND YOUR FRIEND...?

OH...TSUTSUI-SAN... Y-YEAH... IT'S BEEN A WHILE.

YOU...FOUND...?

WELL...WE FOUND AN UNUSUAL CORPSE.

SO, WHAT'S THIS ALL ABOUT...?

OH...

MAKINO THOUGHT MAYBE WE SHOULD GET YOUR OPINION. WHO COULD SHE BE?

YES. WE'RE TRYING TO IDENTIFY IT, YOU SEE.

HER NAME IS AYUMI SUZUKI, AGE 22. CAUSE OF DEATH, STABBING.

SHE WANTS TO BE DELIVERED TO SETA CITY IN SETAGAYA-KU.

...THAT SHOULD BE ENOUGH TO GO ON, RIGHT?

LET'S JUST TAKE THE WHOLE THING TO WHERE THE HEAD WANTS TO GO.

WHAT CAN I DO? YOU EVER TRIED HOLDING A CONVERSATION WITH A RIGHT FOOT?

ENOUGH? THAT'S JUST WHAT THE HEAD WANTS. YOU'VE HARDLY GOTTEN A THING OUT THE REST.

Head) - Ayumi Suzuki (22) wants : To be taken to Seta City in Setagaya-ku

Left Arm Name Unknown wants - Unknown

Right Shoulder Name Unknown wants : To go home

Body Tomoe wants : To be put back together

Right Arm Name Unknown wants - Unknown

Left Leg Name Unknown wants : Help me

Right Foot Untalkative

Well... he's right...

YEAH, KEEP SCRATCHIN' THAT SKIN, AND MAYBE AT LEAST SOME BRAINS'LL GROW. DO YOU KNOW HOW BIG SETA CITY IS?

HOLD ON A MINUTE...I'M GETTING SOMETHING MORE...

132

SHE...
ONE OF
THEM...
WANTS TO
IMAGINE.

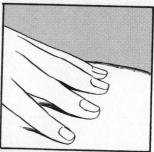

NO...NOT TO
IMAGINE...

IMAG NE
HAIR-MAKE UP
IMAGINE

TO GO TO
"IMAGINE."
WHAT DOES
THAT MEAN?

THEN I CAME UP WITH
THIS *CRAZY* IDEA. I
LEARNED SO MUCH ABOUT
COSMETICS AND
HAIRSTYLING IN MORTUARY
SCIENCE...MAKING THE
BODY LOOK PERFECT.
TECHNIQUES NO ONE ELSE
WOULD KNOW. WHY DON'T
YOU GIRLS COME BY,
WHEN YOU GET
FRUSTRATED LOOKING
FOR SERIAL KILLERS?

WHAT'S THE
POINT? WHEN
I CAME BACK
TO JAPAN, I
THOUGHT I'D
SPREAD THE
PRACTICE HERE.
I FOUND OUT
YOU CAN'T
CHANGE A
SOCIETY'S
HABITS.

I DON'T
THINK I CAN
HELP YOU
WITH THAT.
BESIDES, I
RUN A SALON
NOW...I'M NO
LONGER AN
EMBALMER.

COME ON, MAKINO. WE HAVE TO RUN.

SA-SA-KI? WHERE ARE YOU *GOING*?

COULD WE? I'M SORRY IF WE WASTED YOUR TIME TODAY. I'D LIKE TO MAKE IT UP TO YOU.

WHAT DO YOU MEAN?

WE STILL HAVEN'T EVEN LEARNED WHO DID IT!

WHAT'S THE *MATTER*, SASAKI?

HE DID IT, OF COURSE.

I'M STARTING TO APPRECIATE THE DIFFERENCE BETWEEN WEIRD AND INSANE. DID YOU *LISTEN* TO HIM? I THINK HE *SORT OF* CARES ABOUT NOT GETTING CAUGHT... BUT NOT ENOUGH TO PRACTICALLY INVITE US STRAIGHT-UP TO BE HIS NEXT VICTIMS.

HE DID IT, I DON'T KNOW WHY. I DON'T KNOW IF THERE IS A *WHY* FOR KILLING SEVEN WOMEN AND THEN SEWING TOGETHER THEIR BODY PARTS.

WH... WHAT? WHY WOULD HE...

"SERIAL KILLER?" WHEN DID WE EVER SAY *SERIAL KILLER?* WE NEVER MENTIONED PARTS HAD BEEN SEWN TOGETHER...OTHERWISE, THERE'S ONLY *ONE* BODY IN THAT PHOTO.

YOU KNOW, I DON'T WANT TO GET THE *LAW* INVOLVED WITH OUR BUSINESS. AND DO YOU KNOW WHY?

.....

BECAUSE WE'LL ONLY GET PAID FOR *JUSTICE.*

...HE CUTS HAIR, TOO...?

...NUMATA?

BUT HAS HE REALLY BEEN KILLING PEOPLE?

WELL, NO, CHICKIE. PROBABLY JUST A COINCIDENCE HE'S GOT A STACK OF CORPSES IN THERE!

THAT'S SPACE SOCK, BUDDY!

THE SOCK'S RIGHT. THERE'S FOUR OR FIVE BODIES AHEAD...AND BELOW.

ALL RIGHT... LET'S DO THE JOB, THEN.

NO SENSE BEATING MYSELF UP OVER IT. THAT'S NOT GOING TO HELP.

IT'S LIKE I CAN'T PLEASE ANYONE!

IT'S NOT LIKE I *WANTED* ANYONE TO SEE THAT! IT WAS SO *EMBARRASSING!* THAT WASN'T THE EFFECT I WAS GOING FOR AT ALL!

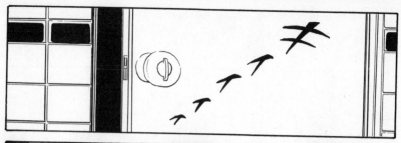

KUROSAGI CORPSE DELIVERY SERVICE.

WH-WHO'S THERE!?

..."CORPSE"?

IF IT'S A HEAD YOU'RE LOOKING FOR, THEN HOW ABOUT *AYUMI'S*? IT'S NOT ORDINARY AT ALL. IT TALKS TO ME, EVEN THOUGH SHE'S DEAD.

--WHO ARE YOU...?

THAT'S--

OUR CLIENTS PAY US. I REALLY DO HEAR THE VOICES OF THE DEAD. I'M AN *ITAKO*, YOU SEE.

WHAT DO YOU WANT FROM ME? MONEY...? IS THAT WHY YOU HAVEN'T GONE TO THE POLICE...?

I DON'T EXPECT YOU'D UNDERSTAND THIS KIND OF ART.

NO...YOU'RE JUST ANOTHER PHILISTINE, IS WHAT YOU ARE.

143

144

THEY ARE
DEAD AND
RATTLING
THE BARS
OF THEIR
CAGE.

145

HA-HA...HOW'D
YOU MAKE
HER MOVE...?

150

152

MIGHT AS WELL CALL THE POLICE. VERY ANONYMOUSLY.

THEY'RE ALL FREE NOW. LET'S GET THE HELL OUT OF HERE, OKAY?

NOT THAT I THINK THEY'LL GET A CONFESSION OUT OF HIM...OR ANYTHING MUCH ELSE.

HA HA HA...

ISN'T THIS...

ALL THOSE BODIES, AND WE DIDN'T MAKE A YEN OFF ONE OF THEM.

KIRIN BREWERY COMPANY · LIMIT

I GUESS THIS KIND OF THING IS GOING TO HAPPEN. WHEN YOU TAKE OFF THE WEIGHT THAT'S HOLDING THESE DEAD DOWN...

...IT SHIFTS A WHOLE LOT OF STRANGE BURDENS ONTO THE LIVING.

CAN'T WE COLLECT A REWARD? WE CAUGHT THE KILLER, AFTER ALL.

YEAH, LET'S DO THAT, AND GET THROWN IN THE LOONY BIN WITH OUR GOOD FRIEND, MR. HAIRDO!

154

3rd delivery: magician of lost love—the end

4th dIvory

九月の雨

september rain

...FOR DAYS.

I FEEL LIKE WE'VE BEEN EATING THE SAME BRAND OF INSTANT NOODLES...

BASED ON NUMATA'S SUGGESTION, WE HAVE, IN FACT, BEEN EATING THE SAME BRAND OF INSTANT NOODLES FOR DAYS.

AND YOU WOULDN'T LOOK GOOD IN A WINDBREAKER. Prada or not.

BUT YOU HAVE SUCH HORRIBLE LUCK WITH CONTESTS, NUMACCHI.

HEY, I CAN'T HELP IT IF I WANT ONE, OKAY?

WITH EVERY STICKER FROM BENEATH THE LID, YOU GET THE CHANCE TO WIN A *FREE* PRADA SPORTS WINDBREAKER!

AND *LOOK* AT ALL THESE WE'VE GOT NOW!

GREAT. LET'S GET STARTED.

I THINK THE COAST IS CLEAR.

YEAH.

OKAY, KARATSU.

I'M JUST JUDGING BY APPEARANCES. CORPSES IN THE WATER CAN BE THE WORST.

THAT DOESN'T MATTER TO HER OR TO ME. I'M HERE TO FIND OUT WHAT DOES MATTER TO HER.

I'M NOT GOING TO CLOSE HER EYES.

THAT'S OUR BUSINESS.

162

MURDER... AN INSURANCE SCAM...IT SOUNDS LIKE A STRAIGHT-FORWARD JOB.

DRIVER'S LICENSE...CREDIT CARDS...NOTEBOOK, AND EVEN THIS GUY YANAGAWA'S *BUSINESS CARD!*

AND WE'VE GOT A LOT OF LEADS. *DAMP* LEADS, BUT *LOTS!*

IF WE'RE LUCKY, WE MIGHT CLEAN UP ON THIS.

MOST NORMAL ONE SO FAR.

YOJI YANAGAWA. HE'S AN ACTUARY IN THE ACCOUNTING DIVISION OF THIRD NATIONAL LIFE INSURANCE.

YEAH, RIGHT. CALL UP A GUY WHO'S JUST COMMITTED MURDER, AND SAY SOME STRANGERS WANT TO TALK TO HIM.

WHAT'S AN "ACTUARY"?

WHY DON'T YOU ASK HIM YOURSELF? WE'VE GOT HIS CELL NUMBER.

COOL!

HE SAYS HE'LL SEE US...

OKAY...YES. YES. REALLY? YES? ONE MOMENT, PLEASE.

HE SAYS HE'LL ONLY MEET US AT A CERTAIN TIME AND PLACE.

HE SOUNDS A LITTLE SUSPICIOUS, THOUGH.

SORRY TO KEEP YOU WAITING. OUR NAMES...? I'M YUJI YATA...

YEAH, WE'RE NOT GOING INTO ANY DARK ALLEYS.

THAT DEPENDS ON THE WHEN AND WHERE.

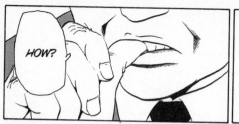

HOW?

THERE'S NO WAY THEY COULD HAVE FOUND OUT.

THEY MUST KNOW. BUT *HOW'D* THEY KNOW?

THIS IS BAD... REALLY BAD.

COULD SHE HAVE TOLD THEM BEFORE SHE DIED...?

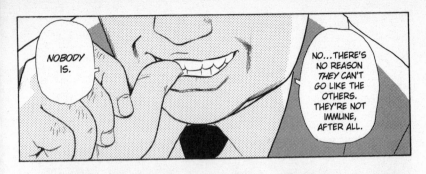

NOBODY IS.

NO...THERE'S NO REASON *THEY* CAN'T GO LIKE THE OTHERS. THEY'RE NOT IMMUNE, AFTER ALL.

HE WANTS TO MEET US UP THERE. DUDE DOESN'T KNOW WE'VE GOT THE BODY.

MAYBE HE WOULD HAVE BEEN MORE CONSIDERATE.

GREAT... MORE BODY HAULING. WE SHOULD HAVE BEEN PIANO MOVERS.

166

NOW *hahh* WHAT WAS IT AGAIN THIS GUY *hahh* DOES FOR A LIVING? DID YOU ASK HIM?

OH *hahh* YES...AN ACTUARY...

hahh
hahh
hahh
hahh

PUT SIMPLY--IN DEFERENCE TO YOU--HE CAREFULLY CALCULATES JUST HOW MUCH OF A FUCK-UP YOU ARE, AND THEN JACKS YOUR INSURANCE RATES ACCORDINGLY!

IT'S A PERSON WHO DETERMINES COVERAGE AND ANNUITY PREMIUMS, RESERVES, AND DIVIDENDS BASED ON ESTABLISHED PATTERNS OF RISK.

WELL I *hahh* CERTAINLY HOPE SO.

WELL *hahh* HE DID ASK A LOT OF QUESTIONS ABOUT US IN RETURN. THINK *hahh* HE'S GOING TO OFFER US A PAYOFF?

I SEE...BUT I'M KINDA *hahh* SURPRISED HOW MUCH HE'S TOLD US ABOUT *hahh* HIMSELF.

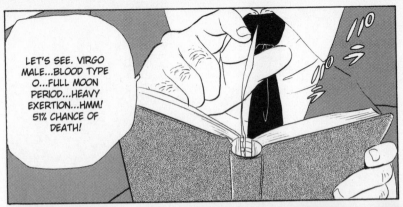

LET'S SEE. VIRGO MALE...BLOOD TYPE O...FULL MOON PERIOD...HEAVY EXERTION...HMM! 51% CHANCE OF DEATH!

ung

hahh

hahh

haa

hahh

ung

ahh ALL OF A SUDDEN...

...IT'S M-MY CHEST...

hahh

hahh

hahh

YATA...? YOU WANT TO REST A MINUTE...?

hahh

hahh

hahh

hahh

169

HUH? INCOMING CALL--?!

NUMATA, QUICK!

I'LL CALL 119!

OH, THAT'S WONDERFUL. I'LL JUST CONTACT YOU AGAIN IN A FEW DAYS.

PLEASE TAKE CARE.

HELLO, THIS IS YOJI YANAGAWA. I REGRET THAT SOMETHING HAS COME UP, AND THAT I WON'T BE ABLE TO KEEP OUR APPOINTMENT THIS EVENING. WOULD IT BE POSSIBLE FOR US TO MEET ON ANOTHER OCCASION?

SOMETHING'S, *ah*, COME UP HERE TOO...LISTEN, C-CALL US BACK, OKAY...?

H-HUH? YEAH ...!

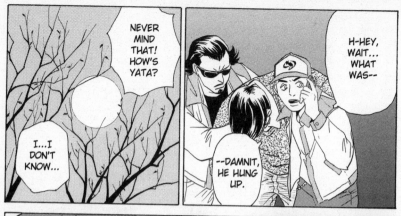

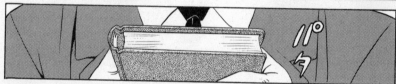

"PLEASE TAKE CARE"...

THAT'S GOOD, ISN'T IT...?

THE DOCTORS SAID THEY WANT TO RUN SOME MORE TESTS...BUT HE SHOULD BE OUT OF THE HOSPITAL SOON, AT LEAST.

I DIDN'T KNOW YATA HAD A BAD *HEART!* BAD *HAND...* YEAH!

IT WAS THE *WAY* HE SAID IT. LIKE HE KNEW SOMETHING HAD GONE WRONG. HEY...PULL OVER, THIS IS THE RENDEZVOUS.

The living one, not the mummy.

STILL TRIPPING ON THAT PHONE CALL? YOU'RE READING TOO MUCH INTO IT. MY GRANDMA ALWAYS TELLS ME THE SAME THING.

カチャ

HE'S ALREADY KILLED ONE PERSON, HASN'T HE? LET'S STAY ON OUR TOES.

WHERE ARE YOU GOING?

WHAT? YOU'RE THINKING HE DID SOMETHING TO *YATA?* HOW COULD HE HAVE GIVEN HIM A HEART ATTACK? WE'VE NEVER EVEN MET THE DUDE.

172

GONNA TAKE A LEAK.

BE CAREFUL. KEEP IT OFF YOUR TOES.

AND THAT INSURANCE MAN ISN'T HERE YET...DID HE FLAKE ON US AGAIN...?

MAN...LOOK AT THOSE CLOUDS. I HEAR THUNDER.

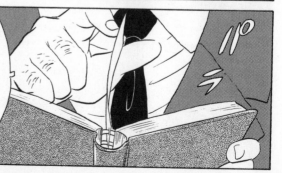

YES...BORN IN GUNMA PREFECTURE...HEIGHT ABOVE 190 CM...LONG WAVY HAIR...LATE SEPTEMBER PERIOD...HILLTOP LOCATION...LIGHTNING STORM IN AREA. AH-HA! 42% CHANCE OF DEATH!

174

NUMATA! ARE YOU ALL RIGHT?

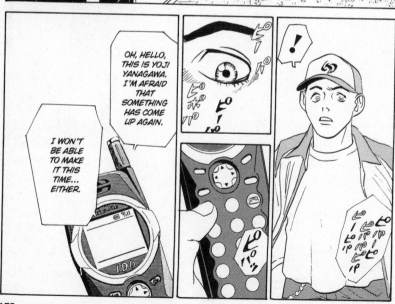

OH, HELLO, THIS IS YOJI YANAGAWA. I'M AFRAID THAT SOMETHING HAS COME UP AGAIN.

I WON'T BE ABLE TO MAKE IT THIS TIME... EITHER.

!

AND LOOK AT YATA HERE! *BACK TO NORMAL!*

YOU KNOW, IT MUST HAVE BEEN ALL MY CLEAN LIVING THAT I GOT AWAY WITH ONLY A FEW BURNS.

Student Cafeteria

OPEN

11AM - 2:30PM

WELL, ANYWAY, THE IMPORTANT THING IS WE BOTH CAME THROUGH OKAY.

YOU THINK SO?

I THINK IT'S BECAUSE YOU WERE INSIDE A CAR. IF YOU'D BEEN OUTSIDE LIKE KARATSU...

NOT THAT HE *CAUSED* IT...IT'S MORE LIKE HE *KNEW* IT WAS GOING TO HAPPEN, SOMEHOW. I MEAN, IF YOU HAVE AN ACCIDENT TWICE WHILE TRYING TO MEET THE SAME PERSON, IS IT REALLY AN ACCIDENT?

And what was that "...tch"?

AND KARATSU... YOU STILL THINK THAT THIS YANAGAWA PERSON SOMEHOW CAUSED ALL OF THIS?

I JUST CAN'T SEEM TO LET IT GO.

WELL...YOU GOT ME THERE...

HOW COULD HE *KNOW* SOMEONE WOULD GET HIT BY LIGHTNING, OR HAVE A HEART ATTACK?

OH, I HAVE SOME MAIL.

HMM, NOW *THIS* IS GETTING INTERESTING ...

SOMEONE ON *CORPSE CHAT* HAS A FRIEND IN THE INSURANCE INDUSTRY... APPARENTLY YANAGAWA HAS QUITE A REPUTATION.

...HM? A FILE?

I'VE BEEN ASKING AROUND ON MY HOMEPAGE ABOUT THAT BODY AND YANAGAWA, BUT...

WHAT'S UP?

WHAT'S THIS?

4	Oichiro Hara	34	Japan Fire	¥25,000,000	
	Katahiko Sugimoto	24	Fuji Fire	¥20,000,000	
	Yoshiyuki Sato	44	Yasuda Fire	¥45,000,000	
	Takashi Morishita	35	Sendai Fire	¥30,000,000	
	Tomoko Miyamura	27	Yasuda Fire	¥25,000,000	
	Seiko Tanaka	40	Dowa Fire	¥50,000,000	
10	Shiho Nishio	33	Mitsui Sea	¥120,000,000	
11	Masayuki Yoshida	22	Mitsui Sea	¥15,000,000	

THIS WAS THE "INSURANCE MONEY" SHE WAS TALKING ABOUT?

SHE AND YANAGAWA WERE SUSPECTED OF RUNNING AN INSURANCE FRAUD RING TO HELP PEOPLE COLLECT ON PHONY ACCIDENTS...EXCEPT THE ACCIDENTS WERE REAL--AND FATAL.

THIS ATTACHMENT SHOWS PAYOUTS THAT WERE MADE IN THE PAST FEW YEARS...ALL TO OUR DEAD CLIENT.

HOW MUCH ?!

YES, AND IT TOTALS SEVERAL HUNDRED MILLION YEN...

THE ONLY COMMON FACTOR IS THAT SHE AND YANAGAWA WERE THE CONTINGENT BENEFICIARIES IN EVERY CASE...

SORRY. HEY, HOLD ON. WHAT KIND OF "ACCIDENTS" WERE THESE, ANYWAY?

KEEP IT DOWN, DUMMY.

No.	Name	Cause of Death
1	Tamiko Utsuki	Car Accident on the Tomei Express
2	Junko Ishikawa	Food poisoning due to Vibrio par
3	Koji Otomo	Collision with another car on Hw
4	Oichiro Hara	Heart attack at a concert at Yo
5	Katahiko Sugimoto	Blood clot while on flight to Br
6	Yoshiyuki Sato	Heart attack at workplace
7	Takashi Morishita	Stroke while asleep at home
8	Tomoko Miyamura	Accidental fall into the rapids of Irima River
9	Seiko Tanaka	Food poisoning due to Streptococcus faecalis
10	Shiho Nishio	Carried off by high waves on O-oi Pier while fishing
11	Masayuki Yoshida	Hit by falling rocks while climbing Yarigeoka Mountain
12	Shinichi Amami	Fall from 8th floor balcony of apartment
13	Yoshitaka Nonoyama	Fall from ride at Fujikyu Highland
14	Koichiro Ochiai	Brain hemorrhage while bathing

...THEY MUST HAVE TOLD THEM IT WAS NECESSARY TO MAKE THE SCAM WORK. WHO ACTUALLY READS THEIR INSURANCE POLICIES, ANYWAY?

YEAH, BUT WHAT ABOUT OUR CLIENT? IF IT WASN'T FOR KARATSU, ANYONE WOULD THINK *SHE* JUST DROWNED. THERE WERE NO SIGNS OF A STRUGGLE ON THE BODY...BUT SHE SAID YANAGAWA "KILLED ME."

FOOD POISONING... AUTO ACCIDENTS... *FALLING ROCKS...?* YOU GOTTA BE KIDDING ME.

AFTER ALL THEIR POLICY HOLDERS DIE IN ACCIDENTS, HIS PARTNER IN CRIME DOES, TOO...AND THEN HE KEEPS IT ALL.

ALL ACCIDENTS, HUH?

NOT JUST INTERESTING ... MORE LIKE FASCINATING.

IT'S ALMOST AS IF HE CAN ARRANGE FOR THEM TO HAPPEN...

IT'S HIM...

IT SEEMS NO MATTER WHAT I DO, I KEEP MISSING YOU!

HELLO, THIS IS YOJI YANAGAWA ONCE AGAIN.

ALL RIGHT. WHERE?

YEAH...WELL, WHY DON'T YOU LET ME PICK THE PLACE THIS TIME, OKAY...?

YOU KNOW WHERE. THE PLACE WE FOUND THE BODY.

Kuro Karatsu
Born Oct. 6, 1978
Northeastern Japan Libra
Bald Blood Type AB
Height about 180 cm Right-handed
No medical history

Numata ... 17, 1975
... long hair

...AHHHH. LET ME SEE WHAT'S A GOOD TIME, THEN.

I'M SORRY. I NEED TO CHECK.

WELL...?

Kuro Karatsu Born Oct.
Northeastern Japan Libr
Bald Blood Type AB
Height about 180 cm Rig
No medical history

Makoto Numata
Born August 17, 1975
Leo Blood type B long hair

SEPTEMBER/OCTOBER
AFTERNOON **10**

RIVERBANK/RIVER/OCEAN **36**

INITIALS K. K. **24**

BORN IN THE NORTHEAST **17**

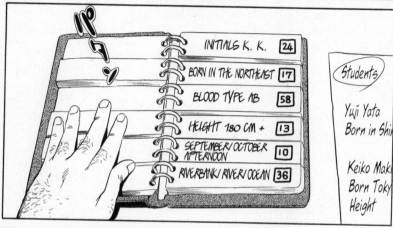

INITIALS K. K. **24**

BORN IN THE NORTHEAST **17**

BLOOD TYPE AB **58**

HEIGHT 180 CM + **13**

SEPTEMBER/OCTOBER
AFTERNOON **10**

RIVERBANK/RIVER/OCEAN **36**

Students

Yuji Yata
Born in Shin

Keiko Maki
Born Tokyo
Height

HEY, I'M WAITING.

Searching...
This may take
a moment.

LET'S SEE...

YOU DO MEAN AFTERNOON, RIGHT? ANOTHER EARLY MORNING'S GOING TO KILL ME.

24 **17** **58** **13** **10** **36**

(Between 4-6PM)

Chance of death is **96%**

YES, THANKS FOR YOUR PATIENCE. HOW ABOUT TOMORROW AT FIVE?

ABOUT HALF A KILOMETER UPSTREAM, WHERE IT'S SAFE.

LIKE MY SECRETS NEED TO BE.

BUT, LIKE A JUDGE, THE LAWS OF *NATURE* CAN *LEGALLY* CAUSE THAT A MAN SHOULD DIE. I LOOK UP SUCH RARE PRECEDENTS, AS IT WERE. AND I ALWAYS WIN MY CASE.

WHAT KIND OF SECRETS WOULD *THOSE* BE? THAT YOU'RE ARRANGING ACCIDENTS FOR PEOPLE AND COLLECTING THEIR INSURANCE?

I DON'T ARRANGE ANYTHING. THAT WOULD BE A CRIME.

ARRANGING....? I DON'T KNOW WHAT THE WOMAN TOLD YOU, BUT YOU'RE QUITE MISTAKEN.

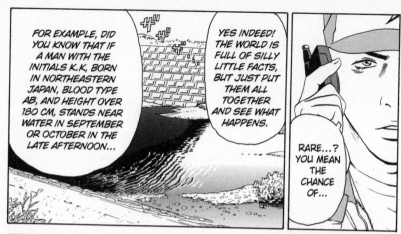

FOR EXAMPLE, DID YOU KNOW THAT IF A MAN WITH THE INITIALS K.K. BORN IN NORTHEASTERN JAPAN, BLOOD TYPE AB, AND HEIGHT OVER 180 CM, STANDS NEAR WATER IN SEPTEMBER OR OCTOBER IN THE LATE AFTERNOON...

YES INDEED! THE WORLD IS FULL OF SILLY LITTLE FACTS, BUT JUST PUT THEM ALL TOGETHER AND SEE WHAT HAPPENS.

RARE...? YOU MEAN THE CHANCE OF...

LISTEN ...

YOU SHOULD HAVE TAKEN OUT SOME INSURANCE, MY YOUNG FRIENDS.

WHAT? WHAT THE HELL ARE YOU TALKING ABOUT...?

....!

YOU SEE, I DISCOVERED HOW EVERYTHING ADDS UP. THESE CHANCES DON'T HAVE A REASON BEHIND THEM--THEY JUST *ARE*. THEY APPLY TO EVERYONE.

TSK! A SUDDEN STORM MUST HAVE OCCURRED UP RIVER. IT LOOKS VERY BAD FOR YOU.

IT'S A GOOD THING I DECIDED TO CANCEL MY GETAWAY TO HAWAII, THEN...AND STAY DOWN HERE...WATCHING THE WATER COVER YOU.

WHY, I CHECK MY *OWN* ODDS CONSTANTLY. THERE'S GREAT DANGER FOR ME FROM A PLANE FLIGHT ALL DAY.

KURO...

I NEED YOUR LIVING HAND TO WORK THROUGH.

...REACH OUT TO ME.

REACH OUT, AND YOU SHALL NOT DIE TODAY.

HAKK

KOFF
KOFF

WHAT...
WHAT
HAPPENED?

NO! GROSS!
I, LIKE,
SWALLOWED
THAT GREEN
SLIME!

barf

ARE
YOU ALL
RIGHT,
MAKINO?

H-HEY...
THEY ALL
MADE IT...

195

WHERE'S HE?

HE JUST... PITCHED OVER THE RAILING ALL OF A SUDDEN, AND FELL IN.

YEAH...

YOU OKAY, MAN?

WELL...HE'S NOT OUR CLIENT. IF HE'S DEAD, HE'LL HAVE TO FIND HIS OWN WAY HOME.

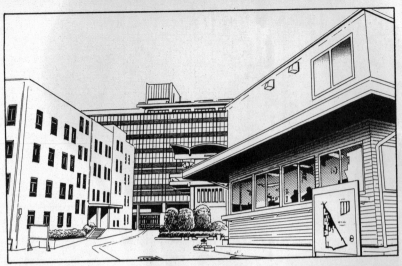

WELL, I STILL DON'T BELIEVE IT.

MURDER BY PROBABILITY, HUH? AND I THOUGHT MATH MAJORS WERE BORING.

SHOW ME HOW IT'S SUPPOSED TO WORK.

...WANTED TO DOUBLE-CHECK, I GUESS.

WELL, YOU *SHOULD*--THE PROGRAM'S RIGHT HERE. LOOK, HE EVEN TOOK HIS LAPTOP TO THE RENDEZVOUS...